I0397038

Disclaimer

This e-book has been written for information purposes only. Every effort has been made to make this ebook as complete and accurate as possible. However, there may be mistakes in typography or content. Also, this e-book provides information only up to the publishing date. Therefore, this ebook should be used as a guide - not as the ultimate source.

The purpose of this ebook is to educate. The author and the publisher does not warrant that the information contained in this e-book is fully complete and shall not be responsible for any errors or omissions. The author and publisher shall have neither liability nor responsibility to any person or entity with respect to any loss or damage caused or alleged to be caused directly or indirectly by this e-book.

Table of Contents

INTRODUCTION

Many businesses and services have jumped on the eBook band wagon and achieved success by publishing them online. Ebooks can be written about any subject or topic you feel your viewers would love to read.

You can even hire others to write your eBooks for you if you'd like. I have found, however, that writing your own eBooks and publishing them on Amazon Kindle is another wonderful and profitable way for you to build any business or service you operate.

Don't freak out if you're not technologically savvy. You don't have to be. In this book, you'll learn how to write a good eBook, add a little "Kindling" and get your business off to a burning success!

WHAT IS A KINDLE?

Unless you've been living in an extremely remote part of the world, you've probably heard of a Kindle Fire, but you might not know exactly what it is and how it operates.

The Kindle is a mini tablet. Technically, it's computer version of the Kindle eBook reader that runs a forked version of Google's Android system.

The cost of a Kindle 'Fire' averages around $159, which means with a price that low, more and more people are going to want to own them. Other great features of the Kindle Fire include:

- 8 GB of internal storage Software
- Android 4.0 operating system
- Access to the Amazon Appstore
- Cloud-accelerated split browser
- Large variety of formats supported such as: Kindle Format 8 Kindle Mobi, PDF, TXT, PRC natively, unrestricted MOBI, PRC natively, Audible/Audible Enhanced AA, AAX, JPEG, PNG, non-DRM AAC, DOC, DOCX, GIF, BMP, MP3, OGG, MIDI, MP4, WAV, and VP8.

BENEFITS OF A KINDLE FIRE

As you can see, the Kindle Fire is an awesome piece of technology. That alone makes people want to have one. It also has many other benefits that make it perfect for your choice to publish your eBook. Never thought of publishing an ebook on Kindle before? Don't worry. If you follow the ideas in this book, you'll be a published author before you know it.

Here are just a few of the totally awesome features to show what a benefit owning a Kindle Fire can do for you:

• Cost effective—As stated above, it is inexpensive. More and more people want to own one because it's much cheaper than the Apple iPad. This gives you a larger customer base. People will be looking for eBooks, and this is one of the greatest platforms of them in the world.

• Simplicity of use—To say "it's so easy a child could do it," would seem like a cliché. Even though it seems that way, it is that easy to use. In fact, it is so easy that many parents purchase them for their children, so it's perfect for every level of eBook you could choose to write. You can write serious adult eBooks or the youngest child eBook and publish it on Kindle.

• Number of Apps—You get many more apps for much less money from Amazon. The selection is huge and they're yours to choose from.

•

- Movies—You can actually play movies from places like Netflix. This may not seem like much for a writer, but it is just another feature that makes someone want to have a Kindle Fire. The more people who own one, the greater the chance of they'll see your eBook.

- Free PDF delivery—You can download files over Wi-Fi at absolutely no cost to you. Many companies charge fees for things like this, but not Amazon.

- Fast Dual-Core Processor—The processor is a state-of-the-art, dual-core processor. It makes it much more powerful. With this you can actually stream music while you're reading books or browse the web while you download videos. It's like multitasking abilities on steroids.

- Battery life—Battery life has always been a problem when it comes to technology. I absolutely hate the life of my cell phone battery. I play a do a bit of work, or at my leisure, play a few games and before I know it, I get that the battery signal is low. With the Kindle, you get a 50% better battery life—that's right—50%. Who could ask for more than a battery with a contrast ratio that good?

- Wi-Fi audible delivery—You no longer need a computer to transfer audible audio books. It can be done over Wi-Fi for a much faster speed. No more lugging that computer around from place to place just so you could download things you felt were important. With the Wi-Fi audible delivery, Amazon has made it easy.

• Improved PDF enhancement—Their PDF reader can now support six contrast options. It also has a cursor so you can highlight words. Contrast options are great for giving anything you create a bright, crisp color.

• Monitoring Download—This allows a user to watch their eBooks download in real time. Don't you have to wait and wait and wait for a download? I know it takes quite a bit of time and it is often time wasted. Being able to watch them download in real time, however, solves that problem.

• Full-Screen Texts—Those reading eBooks can now use the auto-hide feature which gives you more room for texts. This is especially nice for those who are getting older and need larger text to see clearly.

• Two dictionaries are included—You can look up words you want to use in two different styles of dictionaries to inform you of just the answer you were looking for.

• Free Cloud Storage—On many devices, as your memory fills, your machine slows down. I know people who are bad to save things on their computer until it comes to a rapid halt. Then they have to take things off and move them to different files. Or put them on flash drives. With the Kindle Fire, those days are gone, because they give you Amazon Cloud to store all your digital content. Ahhhhh the power of the Cloud!

As you can clearly see, the Amazon Kindle Fire is the most popular tablet of its kind right now for many reasons. Since it's the most popular device for people around the world, it makes excellent sense to publish your eBook there. Sometimes you put your heart and soul into the eBook you want to write. When you do that, you want to give your eBook every opportunity for success that you can, and publishing on Kindle Fire is the best opportunity around. Your book will stay safe in the Cloud as your profits rise to meet it.

RESEARCHING A HOT TOPIC

Perhaps now things are beginning to heat up in your mind and you're beginning to see how valuable publishing on Kindle can be. Maybe you're playing around with the thought to actually write an eBook in your mind, but you just haven't got a clue what to write about. Amazon makes researching hot topics extremely easy for you to do with just a few simple steps:

• First of all, you just simply have to visit http://www.amazon.com/Kindle-eBooks to get started.

• Select a category—Whatever your niche is, simply look for that type of book. You don't have to have a huge business to develop an eBook. As a matter of fact, you don't have to have a business started at all. Maybe you just enjoy baking and would like to publish a cookbook for fast and easy desserts to publish and sell. Simply select the category "cookbooks." You'll see many, but don't get discouraged yet.

• Select a subcategory—A list of subcategories will appear on the left side. Look for something such as "desserts or fast and easy" that applies to whatever it is you're writing about. If you see a lot in that category, you may want try some alternate sub categories, like low fat and delicious.

• View top sellers—This will give you a look at who the top sellers are in the category you want to write in. These are now the people who are considered to be the experts in that particular field. It doesn't mean you can't be the next one.

• Select an eBook—Actually click on one of the eBooks from that list. It can be just any eBook that catches your eye.

• Rank—Look down the page after you click on the book and find the "Amazon Best Sellers Rank." This lets you know who the best sellers at this time are.

• Use the ranks to guide you—Ranks can be a helpful tool for you. They will let you know what was paid in the Kindle Store at the current time of writing. If there have been a lot of eBooks sold, then generally, these are the types of eBooks people enjoy reading and are willing to spend their money on.

Once you've established that people like to buy eBooks based on the niche you've chosen, no matter what that niche is, then you can be confident that if you produce one with quality content, that it will sell. Don't think, "Oh, there's too many and no one will want mine." Think instead—"How can I create an ebook that is so awesome they'll look over others and come looking for mine."

If you think only a beginning eBook writer should publish on Amazon Kindle, you're mistaken. You may be the CEO of your own company that is already doing quite well. Writing and publishing on Kindle can help you grow your business even more.

Don't see how you could write an eBook and use it to improve the success of your company? It really is quite simple. If you are the owner or CEO of a big business, you probably have many areas of expertise that you'd love to be able to share with your customers.

Write down those assets you have and write down the things that your customers ask about the most. Match A to B, and you've got it—there's the content for your eBook. By simply selecting one aspect of your expertise and matching it to the information your customers want, you can determine if books sell well on that topic. If those types are selling, you can begin writing your eBook, and get it out there by promoting it.

Every sale or hit to your book should link to your site. It will increase traffic for your website, and even more greatly improve your chance of business success. It's an awesome way to get your business out there to more people—not only in your area or even your country, but around the entire world. After all, we truly live in a world-wide marketplace.

PUTTING YOUR EBOOK TOGETHER

I hope you're getting excited about the possibility of writing your own eBook and publishing it on Kindle now. You at least know WHY you SHOULD do it. If you're worried about how to do it, it's easier than you may think. Remember, everyone hates first things. I remember the first time I was called to the principal's office. My knees shook the whole way there. I kept going over that very small list of things he may have considered wrong. I was so shook up I didn't think I'd make it through the door. I did, and my mom was waiting for me. I had an appointment she forgot to tell me about!

Was I relieved? The point is, I got myself all worked up over nothing. If you're getting worked up about writing an eBook, you're getting worked up over nothing. It really isn't that difficult.

Many people never take the opportunity to explore the possibility of eBooks because they just don't feel they have what it takes to write a book. When you write eBooks, however, it's a bit different. You're not looking for a 300-page novel. Some eBooks are only about 20 pages long. A good one will probably be at least 30-40 pages. There is, however, no limit. They can be as long or as short as you want them to be or as long or as short as you feel they need to be.

The length often depends on whether or not you're publishing them to sell or publishing them to give away as part of an email marketing campaign, with another purchase, or to special customers. That choice is determined by you. Perhaps you just want to begin writing and write until you've said all you want or need to say to get the message across that you want to portray to your audience. Sometimes, when you begin your first eBook, writing until you've said it all may be the best thing to do. After you've said it all, go back and edit and add more clarity for the reader. Before you know it, you've knocked out more pages than you thought possible. If it's a topic you're passionate about, that won't take long at all to do.

WRITING YOUR EBOOK

Writing in general has a process. It doesn't matter if you're writing an essay for school, a report of some kind, a story, etc. Each one takes a certain process which needs to be done thoroughly. It doesn't matter if it's an article, essay, eBook, or a novel, the general steps are the same. Though eBooks do have a different medium of publication from other books, in most ways, they're alike. For this reason, they're written using the same steps. Here is what you need to do to begin your journey of becoming an eBook author:

• Choose an idea—It does no good to sit down and just try to write your new eBook with no idea what you want to write about. Before you use the above-mentioned steps for researching hot topics, you need to narrow it down a bit.

There may be many things you can do or many aspects of your business you could select to do a book on. It may sound "old school" but still one of the best ways is to get a piece of paper and write down all your options. Just brainstorm and jot down anything you're knowledgeable about or that you think you'd like to write about.

You may not always have the option of writing what you like to write about. The topic may just be handed to you by a superior at times, but for the purposes of this eBook, write down what aspects of that topic you feel you could do best.

Now, you check Kindle for confirmation. You follow the steps listed above see which of those areas have the best-selling books. Then make your final decision from the ones that are selling well on Kindle.

•   Decide who your target market will be—Before you write, you have to know who is going to be reading it. You may be selling it to peers in your industry looking to advance in the field. Maybe you're writing an exercise book for women/men. It could be a cookbook for anyone who loves to cook or a "Macho Man" grilling cookbook. Whoever you feel will benefit from your book is your target market. Those are the ones you write to. You use a writing style which they can relate to and that will bring them in.

•   Create an idea or roadmap—There are many ways to approach an idea and many directions to head in once you get started. Which roads you take will be totally up to you. If you want to write an instructional book, you may decide to write the book and accompany it with a workbook to increase its marketability. The workbook can be extremely important and can also increase your sales. You're giving someone a deal by accompanying your book on the topic with a workbook, so you're giving them more for their money. As you plan the book, plan which sections of the book will go with what worksheet and decide the order and layout of each book. You'd be surprised how easy it is to come up with worksheets. It can even be fun being that creative.

Often, writing an outline of the book will help you stay organized. I will caution you, if you're a "technical" kind of person, which will be further discussed later, try to plan your idea around language that all people can understand.

• Build on the idea—Once your idea and plan are together, it's time to build on it on that idea and get further toward the goal of writing. You've got all the tools you need for success. You know the key concepts you want to get across and what order you want them in. Take each concept you want to portrait in each section of your book and just write a good sentence about it. Then, build on each of these content sentences until you've fully discussed that concept. Then, you simply move on to others.

If you want to write a fiction eBook, you'll have to consider different ideas when creating your plan such as the plot, characters, scene, etc. That will be part of your plan. You'll have to develop each character and design every scene in your head as you prepare to write.

When you write an eBook, it's a lot different than writing the average novel, because it's open to self-publishers at little or no cost to them. The average eBook will probably be too short to print, but definitely long enough that you can develop a valid eBook. That's why it's perfectly fine to even write your eBook using a simple idea. Writing fiction for a child is even available, so just take your best shot.

• Organize the details—The approach you use building on your plan will vary depending on the subject matter. If you're writing a self-help book or maybe your memoirs, the use of an outline works very well. Another way to build is to write down everything you can think of and then draw a web with lines going from each topic.

You've completed brainstorming and writing an outline or a web of ideas, you probably have quite a bit of information about your topic on paper. Look at the information and decide exactly how you feel your book should flow. The order of your book can be important to a reader. It needs to have an even flow and not bounce back from place to place.

Think of what your reader needs to know in the beginning. What do they need to know that is imperative for them to understand before they begin? Put that information at the start of your book. Once your readers get the beginning concepts, they'll be ready to work on more difficult concepts or medium-level concepts.

Save the very difficult concepts for the end. A mechanic would never teach someone to rebuild an engine before he learned to rotate a tire. If you try too hard to push difficult things too early, you may lose them.

If you're writing a self-help eBook on cooking, for example, you can divide each chapter easily by the type of food you're cooking. Some are done by meal such as "Breakfast, Lunch, Dinner, and Dessert." Others do it by the type of food such as "Italian, French,

Mexican, etc." You get the point. Ordering other eBooks may be a little more difficult to do, but having your order thought out is extremely important.

• Write your eBook—Now comes the fun part—writing! You don't need any special equipment to write your book. You can use Microsoft Office Word, or OpenOffice to write it. Don't stress out about what you want to title it or any other elements of the book, just write it.

Every book of any kind has three main sections: Introduction, body, and conclusion. The introduction introduces your topic. The body is the information, story, directions, etc. of your book. The conclusion touches on key points mentioned and leaves the writer feeling the book is complete.

Since the introduction is where they'll start reading, you want to start with something that really catches their attention. Then you "wow" them with your content. In the end, you want to leave the reader with an emotion. It doesn't matter what the emotion is: Happy, proud, sad, a sense of contentedness or achievement, and in some fiction books, even anger. Why? You've made them feel something. When you can write well enough to provoke an emotion from them, you know you've touched them, and that's going to make them glad they read your book. They'll want more, and they'll be happy to let their friends know about your eBook.

There are different ways to write. Many start at the beginning and go straight through to the end. Others like to start in the middle where they're more comfortable with the content and write the beginning and ending when they're satisfied they've gotten their meaning right.

They use their introduction to write into the middle and their conclusion to summarize key points leading out of the middle. Whichever method you choose, you're not committed to it. If it isn't working for you, then just try another until you find which technique works for you. Don't be surprised if you find yourself doing different books differently. Depending on the topic, sometimes it's easier to even start at the bottom and build up.

You're not going to sit down and write your first eBook overnight. It takes time to write a book, even if it is a shorter one like an eBook, it is extremely important that you don't give up on yourself!

If you feel your confidence swaying, and your determination to press on is slipping away, let it go for a bit. Don't try to push yourself into an all-day thing. You may want to set a little bit of time aside each day that is just for writing. You may want to write until you reach a particular word count.

When you reach your goal, then get up from your desk and either stop for the day, or take a break. You'd be surprised how just writing something down, even if you don't feel it's so great, can get your creative juices flowing again.

• Edit—When you finish the book, don't look at it for a few days. After a few days, pick it up and look over it again more critically.

Check the book carefully to be sure you still think all the sections and chapters are ordered and placed in the right order. It's often common to think that some parts of the book would maybe make a little better sense somewhere else. You can cut, paste, and revise until you have it in the perfect order.

Editing takes a good deal of time. Sure, it's not as much time as actually writing, but it's still a good idea to pace yourself. You can edit by a number of pages, number of chapters, or even the number of words—whatever works for you.

Just like sections or chapters needed moved around, you'll find words that you need to rearrange or reword. You may have to move sentences around to keep related ideas together. I know I've sometimes thought, "Why did I put that there?" Just move it around until you have it right.

There's an old saying that "deletion is the soul of editing." If something just doesn't seem to feel right and you can't seem to revise it so it fits, it is often best to just delete it. If you're reading it and you say, "Huh?" Then your reader probably will too. If it is information you feel you have to keep in, just put it away for a while and try to fit it in again in another manner at a later time.

• Detail—When you are confident that the body of your book is exactly what you want, it's time to fine tune and detail your book. There will be things you want to add at this time such as any introduction or conclusion points you feel need added. You'll also probably want a bibliography and maybe a table of contents. The TOC isn't always necessary, but if it's a detailed, self-help or how-to book, it often helps the reader find exactly the sections they're looking for.

Now, you need a very important part of your book…the title. Sometimes, you know right away what you want to title a book. I've written books around great titles. Often times the title may come to you while you're writing the book. Other times, you sit around with an untitled book waiting for a name. Several titles may come to you over the course of time you spend writing the book. Remember when you consider your title, it has to do two things:

1.   Give the reader an idea as to what the book is about
2.   Catch the reader's attention.
3.   Contain keywords your potential customers search for

If you get stuck, take a break. When you come back to it, you may want to play around with the title for a few days. Turn to family or friends you trust and run your ideas by them for their more objective viewpoints. When you're sure you've developed the perfect title, then you can add it to the eBook.

• Credits—Often you use research from other people's works when you write your essay. You'll need to add a bibliography sheet to your book, usually at the back, that gives properly cited information about the author of each source. Often times, your sources are just friends. If that is the case, you should also acknowledge them. There are several ways you can let you know how much you appreciated them, but it is important for you to write a special letter, name each one, and thank them for their help.

• Add your cover—What often draws people to a book isn't the title, but the cover itself. It is a good marketing tool to use when you write your eBook as well. Even though it's a virtual market, it still gives readers a chance to see the virtual cover and causes them to notice you over someone else with similar material.

Often, people will consider hiring someone to design their cover. Other times, they do it themselves. If you feel you can create something that will attract potential buyers, then give it a try. If you can't, maybe you have a friend who may have ideas. If not, there are professionals that will do it. Find one who has work you feel is comparable to what you want and hire them. It will be worth the effort. There are great places on line where you can get the use of "free" images. An example of a free image site is www.sxc.hu. Just remember to do your due diligence and check their terms of use/guidelines for using their images. They'll email what they want written. You can't even use pieces of images that have a copyright. If there's any doubt, make sure you have permission before you use them. It could cause you a lot of problems in the future if you don't.

A lot of people put a lot of effort into their covers and never seem to get them just right. This is where publishing on Kindle can really help you prepare that cover that WOW's the competitions. Kindle has a Cover Creator that can help you create and design your cover. They allow you to either use an image you provide, such as a picture, graphic or custom logo or to choose one of their stock images. You can customize your cover by using their selection of layouts and font sets. The process for doing this is easy. You just follow a few simple steps and you're up and running with your new published eBook:

1.   Select "starting a new" cover—Just click on the existing book title or click on "Add new title" button. Next, you click "Design with Cover Creator." You'll find that in section 4. "Upload Your Cover." Once you do that, the Cover Creator will take over, interface will launch, and you will be provided with directions as to what to do next.

2.   Add the image of your own or from stock images—The image is the focal point of your cover design, so you should select it carefully. You want it to both tell what the book is about and be creative enough to draw a person's eye to it. If you provide your own image, you want to make sure it's an image that is high quality. You must also have total rights to use the image on your cover. Places like www.istockphoto.com and www.sxc.hu have a large number of awesome pictures and graphics you can use.

3.   Select the design you want—There will be 10 design bases you can choose from once you've uploaded your picture. Go

through each base and try your information on it to see what it looks like. Select the one you feel best shows off your information and graphics. After you select one, you can customize it with different layouts, fonts and color schemes. If you you've come this far and still can't find an image you like, don't fret. If you can't find an image you feel portraits your eBook, you can find base designs that allow you to prepare a cover without an image.

4.   Customize the layout—When you choose your base design, you can begin to customize the layout. It's easy to make changes of the fonts, color schemes and layouts of texts. All you have to do when you feel something needs changed is to simply click separately on each part.

5.   Preview your cover and submit it—Once you feel it is complete, all you have to do is click "Preview Cover." You can check to see how it looks in grayscale, color, and even thumbnail modes. Since Amazon uses those thumbnail pictures, it is more important that your picture looks best in the thumbnail mode, not just full scale. If you find something you want to change, simply edit it. When you're pleased with the cover, all you have to do is click "Save & Submit." The Cover Creator will automatically close and load the cover. The cover will be loaded directly into the "Edit book details" of KDP.

You're not stuck with the cover. If at a later date you feel you want to change something, or come across a really cool image you feel is exactly what you were looking for you can simply click "Edit my

Cover." You'll have to finalize again by continuing to the "Rights & Pricing page and then click on "Save and Publish."

If you prefer, you can also outsource the design of your eBook cover to places like www.Fiverr.com. The recommended size of the cover image you should get done is between 1,000 pixels and 2,500 pixels high and between 625 pixels and 1,563 pixels wide. Also, it's recommended that your cover image looks good and is readable if you convert it into a greyscale picture.

FORMAT YOUR BOOK FOR KINDLE PUBLISHING GUIDELINES

When you begin preparing for publishing, there are a few things you should do beforehand:

• Gather all important information—The clearer the information you gather about your eBook, the easier it will be when you get it published. It will also make promoting it easier. For publishing, you'll want to have a separate piece of paper to write on. Write:

1. Title of eBook and the titles of any chapters or sections you have
2. How many sections or chapters you have
3. The word count of the total eBook
4. Using that information develop a list of descriptive terms or keywords you feel relate to the book.

• Know your target market—If you don't know anything else, you need to research to find out who your target market is. Who will buy this book? Who did you write it for? There are a lot of demographics you should consider: age, location, male/female, financial situation, or even if they save or spend their money. It isn't necessary to hire an expert, but you will need to know this information when you get ready to market your book later. Without it it's like tossing daisy petals into the wind and hoping to grow flowers…doesn't happen.

• Pricing—Remember, a publisher should let you price your own book. When you're considering pricing an eBook, generally, the price will turn the most profit if you price them between $0.99 and $5.99 for each copy. It doesn't sound like a lot, but it gets written once, and can be sold for a small amount hundreds of times. The power isn't in the price of the book, it's in the volume of sales. When choosing your sales price, also keep Amazon's royalty structure in mind. To earn for example 70% royalties at Amazon.com, your minimum sales price needs to be $2.99. If you sell it between $0.99 and $2.98, you earn 35% royalties. More on this later on.

HOW TO PUBLISH YOUR EBOOK TO AMAZON KINDLE

You can potentially reach millions of readers across the world by simply publishing your book in Amazon's Kindle store. With eBook sales overtaking traditional book sales at book stores, it makes sense for author to harness the power of Amazon's Kindle store. Besides, what's not to love about ebooks? It's quick and easy to acquire and can be read like a book using a Kindle device or any other ebook reader.

When you publish your eBook, you could become a vendor, but then you would have to deal with all the trips to the postal office to ship out each individual book sold. Instead, joining Kindle Direct Publishing or Amazon Advantage programs make your work a lot easier. You can consider these, but they will be discussed in greater detail at a later point.

Now you're ready to start the publishing process to Amazon Kindle. Some of the above information can seem intimidating, and you may think it is difficult. Believe me, if I can figure out how to do it, then anyone can. Amazon has made it incredibly easy. They have a template you can use to get your book ready for publication at: http://self-publishing-coach.com/kindle-ebook-template.html

We're going to review their publishing guidelines, however, they have a site set up for you at: https://kdp.amazon.com/self-publishing/help

The first thing you need to do is simply go to http://kdp.amazon.com/. Here you can submit your ebook and fill in all the required details. They offer all the tools to create your content and upload it for free. When you publish with Kindle and give them your titles to sell for Amazon Kindle, they will send you payment for each eBook that is sold.

When you're ready to make the eBooks you've written available electronically to the world, you just use Kindle Direct Publishing (KDP). All you need to do is format your book in a one of their support formats. Here are a lot of key factors you should realize about publishing with Kindle:

1.   If you choose the 70% royalty option, there will be no fees such as: sign-up, publishing, etc. You just earn 70% of the cost for each title that qualifies.

2.   Publish one time and sell it everywhere—It will sell automatically on Kindle iPad, PC, Blackberry, iPhone, Mac, and Android phones.

3.   You'll be able to make a connection with the entire author community—They even have author forums if you go to their community pages at: http://forums.kindledirectpublishing.com.

4.   If you have a short content eBook, you can submit the KDP-published as a Kindle Single. Just email it to kindle-singles@amazon.com. You'll need to include a description of the content of the eBook, the ASIN of the title, and their KDP email address.

5.   If desired, you can self-publish the content of your eBook as either a blog or news feed through Kindle Publishing for Blogs.

KINDLE PUBLISHING GUIDELINES

Here are the guidelines required for publishing on Kindle:

• Download the KindleGen program (http://www.amazon.com/gp/feature.html?ie=UTF8&docId=100076 5211)—This program is a tool to help you create eBooks that will be able to be sold through the Amazon Kindle platform. It even gives you a place to download sample ebooks.

•	Agree to the terms of use and begin the download.

•	Next, you download Kindle Plugin for Adobe InDesign —This helps you convert any eBooks or documents into a Kindle Format.

•	You'll also need to install Adobe InDesign before you begin to install Kindle Plugin for Adobe InDesign.

•	If you're a Mac user and you run OS X 10.6.7 or later, then you need to install VeriSign Class 3 Code Signing 2010 CA. This should be installed to the "System" Keychain before you install the plugin.

KINDLE PREVIEWER DOWNLOAD

The Kindle Previewer is very effective tool and you should download it for sure. It helps imitate how books will display on all Kindle devices and applications. It gives you a chance to be sure that the text displays correctly for all orientations or font sizes. It is recommended to help you produce a high-quality Kindle book.

You can get it for either Windows or Mac OSX platforms. Download it at:

http://www.amazon.com/gp/feature.html?ie=UTF8&docId=1000765261

CONTENT GUIDELINES

Following the guidelines set up by Kindle are very important. Everything from your title, cover art, description, and content, has to meet the guidelines. If not, Kindle has the right to decide if they feel the content is appropriate. They may opt to not offer it, or may even terminate your participation in the program if these guidelines aren't met. Here are those guidelines:

• Pornography—Any pornography or offensive graphics showing sexual acts will not be accepted.

• Content that is Offensive—You can probably see by now what kind of content they would seem offensive. It's what you would expect from other respectful publishers.

• Illegal Content or Infringing Content—Laws and proprietary rights are taken very seriously by Kindle. You must understand that just because the content is available all over, doesn't mean you have the right to copy and sell it. You must be responsible enough to make sure your content is not in violation of any laws, trademark, copyright, publicity, privacy or any other types of rights. The responsibility falls on your shoulders, not theirs, but if it is in violation, it will cause you serious problems.

• Non-Exclusive/Public Domain Content—There are many materials, like public domain content, that are free to use for everyone. Kindle doesn't accept content that is available freely unless you are the copyright owner. There really wouldn't be any point in their trying to accept material to sell that is available free online. They accept public domain content, but the content has to be differentiated.

• Customer Experience is Poor—Kindle won't accept books that they feel would provide their customers with a poor experience such as: books with misleading titles, books that are poorly formatted, or if there is any cover art or product descriptions which are misleading. They have the right to decide whether or not your eBook is a poor customer experience.

• Formats—They allow you to convert your draft for many different formats. If you want to get the best results, however, they suggest that you upload in DOC/DOCX or HTML format.

Formatting may seem difficult, but it really isn't. Although they prefer the formats listed above, there are others they accept. Here are descriptions of the suggested formats as well as others accepted:

• Word (DOC, DOCX)—They accept this format, but if you have complex formatting, be aware that it may not convert well. You'll want to use the previewer available so you can check the files conversion. If you are using tables or graphics, you'll need to make sure the conversion shows up properly. If you're using Word, be aware that the font sizes, page numbers, and margin sets won't apply. If you want a page break somewhere, don't just enter a few times to make one. You need to intentionally use the "page break" feature on Word.

That works best when you want to end a chapter because it will make for an easier transition and a better overall reading experience. You'll need to upload the entire book text in one file. They will automatically embed your product image as the cover of the book, so don't include a cover in the file.
If you're using a graphic in Word, then use the "Insert" option to insert the graphic. It won't format properly if you use the copy/paste method.

HTML (ZIP, HTM, or HTML)—You must compress all files into one ZIP file before you upload it if your content contains any images. If you have images and you're using HTML for PC, you need to save it using Web Page, Filtered, (*HTM & *HTML) If you're using a MAC, then you save it using Web Page (.htm) (for Mac) This includes all the images. Then compress them into a ZIP file for upload. If you don't use images, you can simply upload the HTML file without compressing it.

• ePub (EPUB) You should validate your file by going to http://code.google.com/p/epubcheck to be sure it converts properly for Kindle. Kindle will convert ePub files that are unzipped.

• MOBI (MOBI) is the name given to the format developed for the MobiPocket Reader and currently used by Amazon with a slightly different DRM scheme. I personally used this format to publish past eBooks in Amazon KPD. The free Calibre software tool that helps convert your HTML version ebook into MOBI format is available for free for Mac, PC & Linux at http://calibre-ebook.com

• Plain Text (TXT)—You can only use this when your book doesn't contain an image. KDP will convert all text to HTML for you, but if there are any images they will not display in the book.

• Rich Text Format (RTF)—All of these files can be converted.

• Adobe PDF (PDF)—Kindle does accept these files for eBook conversion. If the file contains any special formatting or even some images, they may not export well into the conversion process. Optical character recognition systems often find it difficult to interpret the special formatting that is embedded or the image placement. Many problems such as: irregular bolded texts or page breaks, inconsistent font sizes or text flow, and images that are either missing or oversized. If you have this problem, it is recommended that you convert your PDF to a DOC format.

OTHER PUBLISHING TIPS

The Kindle guidelines are easy to follow to ensure you have a good-quality book to publish there. Others, who have published on Kindle simply love it.

The biggest selling point for any book is going to be quality content. If the book is good, it's more likely to sell. Before they can know its good, however, you have to generate enough excitement for them to want to read it. That's why publishing it properly is so important.

Here are a few other tips you might want to consider when publishing:

• Hire a freelancer for formatting—Although formatting can be done yourself, it can be very frustrating as you try to make sure everything is exactly right. Freelancers are affordable. They can create a file for you. They can also create you an ePub to use on other devices. As with any other person you don't know, be sure to research the freelancer. Check out their previous work and references or testimonials.

•   Pick the right category—You get to select the category for your eBook when you publish onto the Kindle. You get to select a few categories, but not a lot. Remember that this is imperative to get right, because it controls where they will place your book and where it ranks. You have to select the right niche to reach your target market, so choose them carefully. Select the categories you feel readers in your niche will search under.

•   Optimize your cover correctly—You should optimize your cover for the thumbnail size of the Kindle store. Kindle readers like to browse titles of new releases. They'll see your title and cover right away. It will determine if they find it interesting enough to click and download a sample. If your cover only looks good close up, then consider editing it so that it looks good in thumbnail size to catch browsers attention. Also remember that it needs to look good and be readable in greyscale.

•   WOW them with the first few pages—With anything you write this is important, but it's more important with a Kindle release. On Kindle people will download samples. If they read the first few pages and it doesn't grab their interest, they delete them. They may read 20 or more samples and only buy one or two books. They have to be hooked by those few pages. As a good rule of thumb, you should not take 10 or more pages to have your book warm up. You should definitely have them hooked within the first five or they probably will have no interest in your book.

• Targeted advertising—You may not have a large budget, but if you can afford to at all, Kindle Nation Daily is a blog that has advertising its members can pay for. The space goes quickly, so you need to reserve your advertising space months in advance. It has proven to be very effective to many Kindle authors. On Facebook, you can use their paid advertising which can be targeted to those people who "like" Kindle.

• Make sure it is well proofread and edited—If you have an eBook that is filled with typographical and grammatical errors you'll get negative customer reviews which will discourage other readers from purchasing your book.

• Make sure your book description is compelling—This is where the reader gets the chance to learn about your book before they buy. In your description, you have to be able to convince the reader that buying your book will be worth it. Also remember you can use limited HTML in your description such as bolding, italic and lists to make it look nicer to the eye.

• Let the readers know who you are—Be sure you complete your author profile. If you're not sure how to do this effectively, you can use Author Central - http://authorcentral.amazon.com/. Here you can upload a picture of you, add your biography, and view and edit your bibliography. It will even help you create a blog. A blog is a way to directly speak to all of the readers. It only takes a few minutes of your time and it will allow the reader to know more about you and you can begin a rapport with your readers.

- Print-on-demand books—You can create a book that is available both digital and in physical formats if you use CreateSpace. You can do this from the same Amazon.com page. The CreateSpace program is a member of the Amazon group of companies. For your benefit, it has a full selection of tools and services that will help you self-publish. By using it you can make your book available for sale to the many customers on Amazon.com as well as make them available to other channels. What makes it so nice is that your books will always be in stock and available for your customers without any hassle from having to print and ship.

- Video and book trailer uploads—You have the opportunity as a self-publishing author to create video trailers to advertise your books online. You can display them on the Author Pages section. You just have to make a very short video that lets the readers know what the book about and use it to entice them to want more

- Amazon Associates Program—If you join this program, you can earn a 4% more on each sale you drive. This program allows you to create custom links to your books. It also allows you to create interactive widgets. These help to present your book in a more qualified light. Each time a customer clicks on one of those links and they purchase your book, then you get an additional 4% for every sale.

- Backups—You never know when disaster can strike. Your computer could get a virus or even get destroyed or stolen. Don't just rely on your trusty laptop to save your material. Make backups of everything you do. Make sure you have at least one hard copy and make at least two different digital copies and keep them in different places. If you do this, you'll still have your eBook and can recover quickly if something happens.

• 8 ½Xbooks5 done on a word processing program, will only take about 64 pages to be bound. If you write an ebook with more than 30 pages in a Word document, there's a good chance you've created enough for a book.

• Specials—Somewhere in your book, give your readers a little reward. It might be your free report, or it may be a discount on another book or product you have to offer. It's a simple way to say "thank you" that will cause the reader to remember you. Also, consider linking from your eBook to a squeeze page (aka name capture page) where the reader needs to enter his or her email address to collect that reward. This way you can build your own email mailing list that you can then later tell about other Amazon Kindle books you released using your very own Amazon Associate Program affiliate links.

• Invite readers to your site—In your book, maybe in your biography, invite your readers to come visit you on your site. Let them know what you're up to, and show them what the future will hold on the site.

• Call-to-action—The goal is to attract more readers to your site. Every hit to your site increases your search engine optimization and helps you rise in the Google search result pages. It's best if you can put it near the end like maybe the next-to-the-last page. Make sure your site has a great "About You" section where they can learn more about you or your business you're writing about. Always include a picture. It makes it more personal.

PROMOTING YOUR EBOOK

You've gone through all the writing and editing process. You've formatted your eBook properly and have a dynamite cover that will attract the eyes of potential customers, and you've published it on Kindle. Now you just sit back and wait for your sales to go up, right? NO! It's up to you to promote your book. It's up to you to let the world know it's out there and why they should buy it. If you have a budget, like I said above, you can use Kindle paid advertising.

There are also other services that you can pay to help increase your eBook's visibility. If you think you have a book with "best seller" potential, it might be well worth it to pay someone else. For most beginning writer's, however, it will save you more if you promote the book yourself.

You may have money and choose to advertise on Kindle, which is a good thing. You don't, however, want to throw all your advertising efforts in one place. This is especially true if you are a new author. No one has ever heard of you and have no idea who you are or what your book is about. For that reason, you should try some other options. Here are a few:

• Social media—Sites like Facebook, Twitter, LinkedIn, etc are very popular sites. Posts made on these social media sites are seen by a lot of people. If you don't have at least a Facebook account for yourself, you need to create one. They are self explanatory to set up, and only take a few minutes to get up and running. You want to set it up so everyone can be your friend and view your page.

Once you've created your page, post about your book regularly. Get the word out about where it's published and post a link where they can go to buy it. Once you've grown a strong presence on these sites, more and more people will be drawn to your site and your book.

The object with social media is to maximize exposure. Just telling people isn't enough. You need to link it to everywhere they can find it.

• YouTube—YouTube videos are simple to do. You don't have to hire a professional to do it. You can create a short video, usually only about three minutes, introducing yourself and your new book and post it on YouTube. Everything that makes it catchy to a reader will work to attract them to watch your video and learn more.

•   Get yourself out there—When people think real authors are accessible to them, they love it. You can advertise times and have virtual question and answer sessions about the book.

•   Complimentary copies—Google search and find bloggers who review books. Send them complimentary copies of your book and ask them to review it.

•   Be careful with purchasing services—When you're paying for editing or promoting, you want to make sure everything is clear and in writing. Sometimes deals sound so inexpensive, and end up costing you a fortune. If you can't determine what the final cost will be, don't use the service. Find someone you feel comfortable with and you can understand all the fine print.

•   Write another small eBook or report and offer it for free—Everyone likes to get free things. If you offer something free to either your subscribers or those who view your site, you will attract more traffic to your site. Many opt not to do this, because they think writing a report is just too difficult. It is really quite simple if you follow these simple steps:

1. Use a simple word processing program like MS Word

2. Gather several articles you've written

3. Select a few you feel go together and put them in an order that will make sense to the reader.

4. Make sure each concept flows with the next concept

5. Find ways to connect them.

6. Have good sized margins of at least one inch on both the right and left. This will make it easier for people to read.

7. Make sure all the articles are in the same font. You want to use at least 11-12 point fonts because people of all ages need that to be able to read the book. Both Ariel and Verdana have been found easier to read than Times New Roman.

8. Add a few pictures throughout the document. Don't just throw in clip art. That isn't made for professional use, only for personal use. You cannot sell it commercially. Find sites with free pictures and/or art work and use those with the proper credit notations.

9. Have larger, bolder title and chapter titles—If you underline a title, a lot of people will just try to click on it. Instead, use bold or color headings. Create a simple, eye-catching cover page and the report is complete.

You've created something simple and effective that you can give away in a few hours time. It will attract people to you when they're looking for your topic and see that it's "FREE." Then, you can have the link on your site where they can buy your book. If you do a good report, they'll be interested enough to take a look at your book. If they like the way that looks, they'll buy it too.

Once you've done all that, you have a product you can share with possible affiliate programs to help you promote your product in return for a commission, or for your promoting their product on your site. As long as the two are complimentary, it usually works well.

HOW TO DETERMINE THE SALE AMOUNT OF YOUR EBOOK

You were given the opportunity to think about how much you wanted to charge for your eBook earlier. It is important that you decide which way you want to go.

Kindle offers you two royalty options when you publish yourself. They are 35% and 70%. The 35% royalty applies to sales in any territories. The 70% option applies to the territories of Andora, Austria, Belgium, Canada, France, Germany, Italy, Liechtenstein, Luxembourg, Monaco, San Marino, Switzerland, Spain, and the United Kingdom including Guernsey—Jersey and Isle-of-Man, the United States and the Vatican City

If you have chosen 70% then sales outside of the above territories will be paid at the 35% royalty rate.

 If you select the 70% option you should also note that the list price on Amazon must be at least 20% lower than any other publisher offering the digital or physical version of your book.

If you have an eBook that is mainly from Public Domain work, you can only expect to receive the 35% option.

Amazon does have a minimum and maximum price list. If you select the 35% option your book must be priced between a certain set amounts (the minimum price is higher if your book is greater than 3mb in size)

You need to consider what is an appropriate price for a book in your chosen category. This will have shown up in the research you did earlier on in the challenge.

If you price your book too low then you may find it is not taken as a credible offering within the category, if you price your book too high you may find you simply are too expensive compared to your competitors.

Kindle allows you to update the pricing on your book at any time once it has been published, but bear in mind it can take up to 24 hours for a price change to become effective.

Today's challenge is to decide the initial selling price for your book. sites across the Web.

TRACKING YOUR AMAZON KINDLE SALES

Knowing how much you sell on Amazon is probably very important to you, especially if it's your first book and you're all excited about it. There are several ways on Amazon to monitor your sales. If you have print books Amazon has ordered through you or if you have a Kindle Direct account, you can track in real time.

DIRECT REAL TIME

You can check your sales updates reports through both Kindle Direct Publishing and Amazon Advantage programs. All you have to do is log onto your account. You can check out your account as often as you want. Once a day is common, but you may want to check it more if you're running a campaign of some kind, have an ad running, are mentioned on someone else's site such as an affiliate site, or if you've created a blog post that mentions your book.

Other publishers often only give you monthly statements and they send them about three weeks into the next month, so it takes a long time to actually see your results. With Amazon, you can even track print sales through many of their features. They always offer ways to estimate your sales.

INDIRECT TRACKING

Indirectly, you can track your real-time sales in two ways. These are either by tracking the in-stock numbers or you can do it by tracking sales rank. You can find both of these on your Amazon book page. That is the page all of your potential customers can view. These numbers won't mirror your sales exactly, but they can give you a good idea of how well your sales are going.

Since Amazon has a very large number of books, they can't keep inventory of books that are slow sellers. If you have a self-published book, it probably falls into that category. Because of this, they will stock just enough as they anticipate your sales to be during that period of time. They base it on previous sales and only reorder when the inventory is low.

They do, however, entice people who browse to buy the book with statements like, "Order soon, only 2 left in stock." This helps you in tracking. You can check to see if the inventory is changing at all.

You can use the in-stock numbers to let you know how many they have in stock. It will say something like "10 New in stock now" when they order new books from the distributor.
There are a few disadvantages to using the in-stock statistical method.

• They'll only list the number left in stock when that number is low. If you don't know how many they ordered in the first place, you can't figure out how many books they've sold.

• You can only use the "in stock" number if you have a printed book. If your book is an eBook, you can't track this way at all.
If you use the Amazon Best Sellers Rank, you can also indirectly track sales. You just have to scroll down until you find your book. There will be a separate page for paperback, hardcover, and Kindle. Find the Product Details section. Go to the end of it, and you can see what your sales rank is for your book.

You should know that this isn't based on just sales of your book. It also takes into account sales of all books that are in that category. If you see 1,000, that's awesome, but a ranking of 100,000 isn't in the Kindle market.

If other books in your category are selling quickly and yours aren't, your number goes up instead of down. It's not what you want. Your rank goes up when you have more sales relative to the category than other books. They update the ranks hourly.
You should also set up an Author Central account. It's simple to do, and it will let you see sales information that no one else can see. It only goes to you.

Another way is by the Nielsen BookScan. You can find this in the Amazon Author Central tools. It gives you data for sales of printed books for a period of 4-8 weeks. It's close to real time and reflects sales of the prior week. It will also show you where they were from geographically. There may be a few sales that don't show up, but it still gives you an idea of how well everything is going and where your books are selling.

The BookScan report enables authors to learn about their sales close to the time they occur. It's a useful tracking tool if the company that produced your book door not post sales for a month or two. Both Kindle Direct Publishing and Amazon Advantage programs continuously update sales reports, which you can easily accessible logging into your account. You can log onto your Kindle account at least once a day, more frequently when you have an ad running or a new guest blog post that mentions your books.

Other promotion company report contents monthly and run about three months into the next month before you see last month's reports. This causes you not to see your reports for sometimes two months. This makes it difficult at best to track. You can, however, indirectly track print sales through several Amazon features, which offer ways to estimate recent sales. Author Central also provides graphs of your Amazon Best Sellers Rank history for the past four or eight weeks. The separate graphs for each format of your book offer a visual way to compare print and e-book performance.

GATHERING SALES INFORMATION AND USING IT FOR PROMOTIONAL PURPOSES

We have discussed how important the entire process is from beginning to end, everything has to be given your very best work and care. We can't stress enough, however, that creating the perfect book means nothing if you don't take an active part in promoting your book. There are various types of promotion listed in this book, and you should definitely begin to explore each. Try a few different methods at the same time and alternate them weekly. Soon, you'll find the one, or group of ones that will work for you. Remember to get yourself out there. Do guest blogs or webinars. You can often find affiliates who will have you interview them about the eBook and then they will offer to interview you about your book and future plans. Blog posting, webinars, or even mentions of friends public sites can do you the world of good. Then if you add a paid advertisement to the mix, tracking sales results is an excellent way to learn which methods work best.

Viewing your Promotion Results

At a time when you are not doing any promotion, follow your sales figures to establish a baseline. The sales during this period can probably be attributed to word of mouth and search engine hits rather than your intentional efforts.

Be especially watchful in tracking your sales when you are paying for an ad or other type of promotion. A potential customer may not stop what he/she is doing to order a book but will wait until a convenient time. Follow the sales of all of your book's formats. You may have linked to the Kindle version, but a reader may prefer a print copy.

You may often find an increase in your sales if you have a guest blog. They often come through self-ran ads. You can Google your title to see if your book is mentioned. If you don't see something…do it again. Look at all the search results and see if you can even find a mention of your book. Sometimes you may see where someone has asked a question on a blog or twitter remark. If so, take the time to send them a thank you and answer them.

Plan Future Promotions

Now that you know all about your promotion efforts and how they have lead to sales, you're ready to do more. You can better plan now how to spend the balance of your money and your important time you can plan how best to spend your time and money promoting your book.

Guest blogs and webinars won't always generate great sales for your books, but they do allow you to put the titles of your books into visitors' minds, take little effort, and cost nothing. In other words, you may not have gained much by doing it, but you didn't lose anything either.

When it comes to an ad that is paid that is a different story. If you don't see an up flow in sales, you may think twice before continuing or repeating the advertisement.

Keep track of your sales over time. Look at your sales closely to see if they peak in certain months. If they do, then you'll want to remember those months they peak in certain months, concentrate your promotion to hit buyers at or just before the peak. Visiting Amazon pages and looking for related books to see if their sales ranks improve at certain times.

Plan a virtual or life book tour using your sales information available through Amazon's Author Central, to plan a virtual or live book tour. Target locations where your book has already found an audience.

Publicize the events—Create publicity notices and send them to bookstores, libraries, reading clubs or other organization you feel would enjoy attending.

Schedule visits to your home area or the area mentioned in your book. Schedule book signings, readings, and speeches. Sometimes your book will take off in one area and not others. If your readers are from out west, say Colorado. Search for the type of reader in that area who is reading your books. Work with other writing groups, organizations or libraries to set up internet conferences with those readers. You can even go there and set up the same events you did in your local area.

If you keep track of your sales, remember...don't be fooled! You can absolutely succeed as a self-published author.

AMAZON CONTACT SERVICES

Amazon doesn't just sign you up and forget about you. They've given you the tools you need to help you publish your new eBooks. They offer you the use of their tools to help you get your eBook published. With the continued rise of all the many social networking sites, it opens up the world to have the opportunity to view your eBook. There'll never be such a type of available/FREE or minimal cost advertising for which you can promote.

If you have a problem with anything in the book publishing process, Amazon KDP has help sheets to help you. They also have good customer care service, so simply contact them and explain what problems you've had and they will help you to correct them.

Just picture this, a family has gathered around the fireplace after dinner for family reading night. Maybe they call it Kindling Night. They have their Kindles out and ready, but instead of just any other author, tonight... one of them is reading the book YOU wrote! Doesn't that make you feel great?

CONCLUSION

When it comes to publishing your own Kindle eBook, it doesn't need to be hard.

When you've published your first Kindle eBook, don't just leave it, take action and start spreading the word about it. As they say, put in the hard yards now and reap the benefits down the future. The same goes for a Kindle business.

If your first Kindle eBook flops, don't give up. Get back up and try again.

Follow the steps and guidelines in this eBook, and you'll be on your way to Kindling Success!

www.ingramcontent.com/pod-product-compliance
Lightning Source LLC
Chambersburg PA
CBHW061218180526
45170CB00003B/1061

*9 7 8 1 5 4 5 1 4 1 9 6 0 *